NONSENSE SONGS

Edward Lear

ILLUSTRATED BY
BEE WILLEY

NONSENSE SONGS

Orion
Children's Books

To my father

First published in Great Britain in 1996
by Orion Children's Books
a division of the Orion Publishing Group Ltd
Orion House
5 Upper St Martin's Lane
London WC2H 9EA

A catalogue record for this book is available from the British Library
Printed in Italy
Designed by Dalia Hartman

THE OWL AND THE PUSSYCAT

The Owl and the Pussy-Cat went to sea
    In a beautiful pea-green boat:
They took some honey, and plenty of money
    Wrapped up in a five-pound note.

The Owl looked up to the stars above,
And sang to a small guitar,
"O lovely Pussy, O Pussy, my love,
What a beautiful Pussy you are,
You are,
You are!
What a beautiful Pussy you are!"

Pussy said to the Owl, "You elegant fowl,
How charmingly sweet you sing!
Oh! let us be married; too long we have tarried:
But what shall we do for a ring?"

They sailed away, for a year and a day,
    To the land where the bong-tree grows;
And there in a wood a Piggy-wig stood,
    With a ring at the end of his nose,
            His nose,
            His nose,
    With a ring at the end of his nose.

"Dear Pig, are you willing to sell for one shilling
    Your ring?" Said the Piggy, "I will."
So they took it away, and were married next day
    By the Turkey who lives on the hill.

7

They dined on mince and slices of quince,
Which they ate with a runcible spoon;
And hand in hand, on the edge of the sand
They danced by the light of the moon,
The moon,
The moon,
They danced by the light of the moon.

THE JUMBLIES

They went to sea in a sieve, they did;
  In a sieve they went to sea:
In spite of all their friends could say,
On a winter's morn, on a stormy day,
  In a sieve they went to sea.
And when the sieve turned round and round,
And every one cried, "You'll all be drowned!"
They called aloud, "Our sieve ain't big;
But we don't care a button, we don't care a fig:
  In a sieve we'll go to sea!"

Far and few, far and few,
  Are the lands where the Jumblies live:
Their heads are green, and their hands are blue;
  And they went to sea in a sieve.

They sailed away in a sieve, they did,
  In a sieve they sailed so fast,
With only a beautiful pea-green veil
Tied with a ribbon, by way of a sail,
  To a small tobacco-pipe mast.
And every one said who saw them go,
"Oh! won't they be soon upset, you know?
For the sky is dark, and the voyage is long;
And, happen what may, it's extremely wrong
  In a sieve to sail so fast."

Far and few, far and few,
    Are the lands where the Jumblies live:
Their heads are green, and their hands are blue;
    And they went to sea in a sieve.

The water it soon came in, it did;
    The water it soon came in:
So, to keep them dry, they wrapped their feet
In a pinky paper all folded neat;
    And they fastened it down with a pin.

11

And they passed the night in a crockery-jar;
And each of them said, "How wise we are!
Though the sky be dark, and the voyage be long,
Yet we never can think we were rash or wrong,
   While round in our sieve we spin."

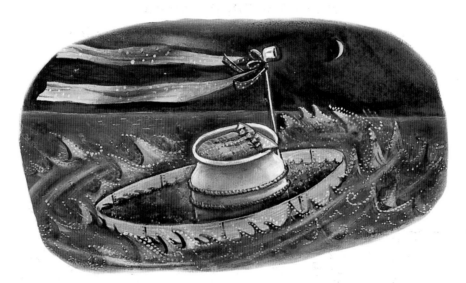

Far and few, far and few,
   Are the lands where the Jumblies live:
   Their heads are green, and their hands are blue;
    And they went to sea in a sieve.

And all night long they sailed away;
And when the sun went down,
They whistled and warbled a moony song
To the echoing sound of a coppery gong,
In the shade of the mountains brown.
"O Timballoo! How happy we are
When we live in a sieve and a crockery-jar!
And all night long, in the moonlight pale,
We sail away with a pea-green sail
In the shade of the mountains brown."

Far and few, far and few,
  Are the lands where the Jumblies live:
Their heads are green, and their hands are blue;
  And they went to sea in a sieve.

They sailed to the Western Sea, they did, –
  To a land all covered with trees:

And they bought an owl,

and a useful cart,

And a pound of rice,

and a cranberry tart,

And a hive of silvery bees;

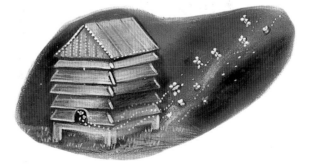

And they bought a pig,

and some green jackdaws,

And a lovely monkey with lollipop paws,

And forty bottles of ring-bo-ree,

And no end of Stilton cheese.

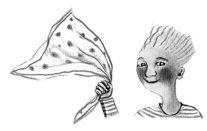 

Far and few, far and few,
  Are the lands where the Jumblies live:
Their heads are green, and their hands are blue;
  And they went to sea in a sieve.

And in twenty years they all came back, –
  In twenty years or more;
And everyone said, "How tall they've grown!
For they've been to the Lakes, and the Torrible Zone,
  And the hills of the Chankly Bore."

And they drank their health, and gave them a feast
Of dumplings made of beautiful yeast;
And every one said, "If we only live,
We, too, will go to sea in a sieve,
   To the hills of the Chankly Bore."

Far and few, far and few,
   Are the lands where the Jumblies live:
Their heads are green and their hands are blue;
   And they went to sea in a sieve.

THE POBBLE WHO HAS NO TOES

The Pobble who has no toes
   Had once as many as we;
When they said, "Some day you may lose them all;"
   He replied, "Fish fiddle de-dee!"
And his Aunt Jobiska made him drink
Lavender water tinged with pink;
For she said, "The world in general knows
There's nothing so good for a Pobble's toes!"

19

The Pobble who has no toes,
    Swam across the Bristol Channel;
But before he set out he wrapped his nose
    In a piece of scarlet flannel.

For his Aunt Jobiska said, "No harm
Can come to his toes if his nose is warm;
And it's perfectly known that a Pobble's toes
Are safe – provided he minds his nose."

The Pobble swam fast and well,
    And when boats or ships came near him,
He tinkledy-binkledy-winkled a bell
    So that all the world could hear him.

And all the Sailors and Admirals cried,
When they saw him nearing the further side, –
"He has gone to fish, for his Aunt Jobiska's
Runcible Cat with crimson whiskers!"

But before he touched the shore, –
  The shore of the Bristol Channel,
A sea-green Porpoise carried away
  His wrapper of scarlet flannel.

And when he came to observe his feet,
Formerly garnished with toes so neat,
His face at once became forlorn
On perceiving that all his toes were gone!

And nobody ever knew,
　From that dark day to the present,
Whoso had taken the Pobble's toes,
　In a manner so far from pleasant.

Whether the shrimps or crawfish grey,
Or crafty Mermaids stole them away,
Nobody knew; and nobody knows
How the Pobble was robbed of his twice five toes!

The Pobble who has no toes
    Was placed in a friendly Bark,
And they rowed him back, and carried him up
    To his Aunt Jobiska's Park.
And she made him a feast, at his earnest wish,
Of eggs and buttercups fried with fish;
And she said, "It's a fact the whole world knows,
That Pobbles are happier without their toes."

THE QUANGLE WANGLE'S HAT

On the top of the Crumpetty Tree
   The Quangle Wangle sat,
But his face you could not see,
   On account of his Beaver Hat.
For his Hat was a hundred and two feet wide,
With ribbons and bibbons on every side,
And bells, and buttons, and loops, and lace,
So that nobody ever could see the face
     Of the Quangle Wangle Quee.

The Quangle Wangle said
  To himself on the Crumpetty Tree,
"Jam, and jelly, and bread
  Are the best of food for me!
But the longer I live on this Crumpetty Tree
The plainer than ever it seems to me
That very few people come this way
And that life on the whole is far from gay!"
  Said the Quangle Wangle Quee.

But there came to the Crumpetty Tree
   Mr and Mrs Canary;
And they said, "Did ever you see
   Any spot so charmingly airy?
May we build a nest on your lovely Hat?
Mr Quangle Wangle, grant us that!
O please let us come and build a nest
Of whatever material suits you best,
    Mr Quangle Wangle Quee!"

And besides, to the Crumpetty Tree
Came the Stork,

the Duck,

and the Owl;

The Snail

and the Bumble-bee,

The Frog

and the Fimble Fowl
(The Fimble Fowl, with
a Corkscrew leg);

And all of them said, "We humbly beg
We may build our homes on your lovely Hat,
Mr Quangle Wangle, grant us that!
Mr Quangle Wangle Quee!"

And the Golden Grouse came there,

And the Pobble who has no toes,

And the small Olympian bear,

And the Dong with
a luminous nose.

And the Blue Baboon who
played the flute,

And the Orient Calf from
the Land of Tute,

And the Attery Squash,

and the Bisky Bat, –

All came and built on the lovely Hat
   Of the Quangle Wangle Quee.

And the Quangle Wangle said
   To himself on the Crumpetty Tree,
"When all these creatures move
   What a wonderful noise there'll be!"

And at night by the light of the Mulberry moon
They danced to the Flute of the Blue Baboon,
On the broad green leaves of the Crumpetty Tree,
And all were as happy as happy could be,
　　With the Quangle Wangle Quee.